The League of Nations: The Controversial History of the Failed Organization that Preceded the United Nations

By Charles River Editors

A picture of a 1928 meeting of the League of Nations

About Charles River Editors

Charles River Editors provides superior editing and original writing services across the digital publishing industry, with the expertise to create digital content for publishers across a vast range of subject matter. In addition to providing original digital content for third party publishers, we also republish civilization's greatest literary works, bringing them to new generations of readers via ebooks.

Sign up here to receive updates about free books as we publish them, and visit Our Kindle Author Page to browse today's free promotions and our most recently published Kindle titles.

Introduction

Ville Oksanen's picture of the Palace of Nations

The League of Nations

"The program of the world's peace, therefore, is our program; and that program, the only possible program, as we see it, is this: 1. Open covenants of peace, openly arrived at, after which there shall be no private international understandings of any kind but diplomacy shall proceed always frankly and in the public view." – President Woodrow Wilson

"I have loved but one flag and I can not share that devotion and give affection to the mongrel banner invented for a league." – Henry Cabot Lodge

"The League of Nations is the greatest humbug in history. They cannot even protect a little nation like Armenia. They do nothing but pass useless resolutions." – David Lloyd George

The United Nations is one of the most famous bodies in the world, and its predecessor, the League of Nations, might be equally notorious. In fact, President Woodrow Wilson's pet project was controversial from nearly the minute it was conceived.

At the end of World War I, Wilson's pleas at the Paris Peace Conference relied on his Fourteen Points, which included the establishment of a League of Nations, but while his points were mostly popular amongst Americans and Europeans alike, leaders at the Peace Conference largely discarded them and favored different approaches. British leaders saw their singular aim as the maintenance of British colonial possessions. France, meanwhile, only wanted to ensure that Germany was weakened and unable to wage war again, and it too had colonial interests abroad that it hoped to maintain. Britain and France thus saw eye-to-eye, with both wanting a weaker Germany and both wanting to maintain their colonies. Wilson, however, wanted both countries to rid themselves of their colonies, and he wanted Germany to maintain its self-determination and right to self-defense. Wilson totally opposed the "war guilt" clause, which blamed the war on Germany.

Wilson mostly found himself shut out, but Britain and France did not want American contributions to the war to go totally unappreciated, if only out of fear that the U.S. might turn towards improving their relations with Germany in response. Thus, to appease Wilson and the Americans, France and Britain consented to the creation of a League of Nations. However, even though his participation in the crafting of the Treaty of Versailles earned him a Nobel Prize that year, Wilson soon learned to his consternation that diplomacy with Congress would go no better than his diplomacy with European leaders. The only major provision that Wilson achieved in Europe, the League of Nations, was the most controversial in the United States. Both aisles of Congress had qualms with the idea, believing it violated the Constitution by giving power over self-defense to an international body. Other interests in the United States, especially Irish-Americans, had now totally turned against Wilson. The President's interest in national self-determination extended to many European countries, including Hungary, Poland, Czechoslovakia and Belgium, but it excluded one critical country: Ireland, a country currently embroiled in a revolution against Great Britain. Worse, Irish-Americans thought the League of Nations would harden Anglo control of global institutions.

Simply put, Wilson returned home to find many Americans weren't buying the League of Nations. While the Senate was able to build a slim majority in favor of ratification, it could not support the necessary two-thirds majority. Too many were skeptical of the Treaty, especially given Europe's inability to adopt the remainder of Wilson's Fourteen Points. As a result, ironically, the United States didn't join the League of Nations, which would last only about 25 years. While it would attempt to resolve some territorial disputes, it simply proved too weak to prevent international aggression, primarily among the Axis Powers in the buildup to World War II. Thus, the League's greatest legacy ended up being its dismal failure to prevent World War II and ensure that World War I had truly been the "war to end all wars," as originally intended.

Although the League of Nations was short-lived and clearly failed in its primary mission, it did essentially spawn the United Nations at the end of World War II, and many of the UN's structures and organizations came straight from its predecessor, with the concepts of an

International Court and a General Assembly coming straight from the League. More importantly, the failures of the League ensured that the UN was given stronger authority and enforcement mechanisms, most notably through the latter's Security Council, and while the League dissolved after a generation, the UN has survived the last 70 years.

The League of Nations: The Controversial History of the Failed Organization that Preceded the United Nations looks at the history of the short-lived league. Along with pictures of important people, places, and events, you will learn about the League of Nations like never before.

The League of Nations: The Controversial History of the Failed Organization that Preceded the United Nations

About Charles River Editors

Introduction

    Chapter 1: Forerunners to the League and the Start of World War I

    Chapter 2: We Must Bring About a League or a Union of Nations

    Chapter 3: There Must Be a Union Which Has Force Behind It

    Chapter 4: A Practical Necessity

    Chapter 5: No Right To Run Away From Its Obligations

    Chapter 6: It Has Been Decided to Bury It and Start Afresh

Online Resources

Bibliography

Chapter 1: Forerunners to the League and the Start of World War I

"This is an age of unions. Not merely in the economic sphere…but law, medicine, science, art, trade, commerce, politics and political economy—we might add philanthropy—standing institutions, mighty forces in our social and intellectual life, all have helped to swell the number of our nineteenth century Conferences and Congresses. It is an age of Peace Movements and Peace Societies, of peace-loving monarchs and peace-seeking diplomats. … Men are working together, there is a newborn solidarity of interest, but rivalries between nation and nation, the bitternesses and hatreds inseparable from competition are not less keen; prejudice and misunderstanding not less frequent; subordinate conflicting interests are not fewer, are perhaps, in view of changing political conditions and an ever-growing international commerce, multiplying with every year. The talisman is, perhaps, self-interest, but, none the less, the spirit of union is there; it is impossible to ignore a clearly marked tendency towards international federation, towards political peace. This slow movement was not born with Peace Societies; its consummation lies perhaps far off in the ages to come. History at best moves slowly. But something of its past progress we shall do well to know. No political idea seems to have so great a future before it as this idea of a federation of the world. It is bound to realise itself some day…." - Introduction to the 1917 English translation of *Perpetual Peace: A Philosophical Sketch* by Immanuel Kant

In 1795, the famous philosopher Immanuel Kant posited the idea that peace might be achieved if the nations of the world got together to agree to solve the disagreements peaceably through cooperation, and in that manner world peace could be maintained. Ironically, Kant formulated the idea in the midst of the violent French Revolution, and near the start of the Napoleonic Era, which would lead to a series of conflicts among the great European powers on the continent for decades.

Kant

Following the end of the Napoleonic Wars, Austria, Prussia, Russia, France and Great Britain formed a pact called the Concert of Europe. Part of the Congress of Vienna, the European powers aimed to achieve at least an uneasy peace across Europe, but the Europeans continued to conduct business as usual, spending much of the 19th century engaged in imperialism across the world. The natural response of the various European nations was to establish alliances that would maintain at least a balance of power.

Although a couple of wars were fought on the European continent during the 19th century, an uneasy peace was mostly maintained across the continent for most of the 19th century after Napoleon, but despite this ostensible peace, the Europeans were steadily conducting arms races against each other, particularly Germany and Britain. Britain had been the world's foremost naval power for centuries, but Germany hoped to build its way to naval supremacy. The rest of

Europe joined in on the arms race in the decade before World War I started.

In 1878, the Great Powers signed the Treaty of Berlin, a document intended to pacify the Balkans, where the Ottoman Empire had been forced to use brutal force to suppress rebellion on more than one recent occasion. Among other clauses, the Treaty empowered the Austro-Hungarian Empire to take nominal charge of the Bosnia District of the Ottoman Empire, although it officially remained Turkish territory. At the same time, the Treaty also acknowledged the sovereignty of the Principality (later the Kingdom) of Serbia, under the aegis of King Milan Obrenovic, whose family was closely connected to Austrian Emperor Franz Joseph's family and was well-liked at court. This diplomatic connection helped ensure stability within a notoriously volatile region; administrative power passing to a European power with a Christian government and a long-term vested interest in the East helped quell much of the turmoil to which the Balkans had been subject to under Ottoman rule, while Serbia provided a useful and friendly bulwark to calm any unrest which might occur.

However, things went disastrously awry in 1903 when a military coup took place in Serbia. A group of officers and soldiers, commanded by Dragutin Dimitrijević, assaulted the Royal Palace under cover of darkness. After brutal room-to-room fighting, they managed to capture General Laza Petrovic, commander of the Royal Bodyguard, who had escorted the royal family to the safety of a hidden "panic room" while his soldiers held off the attackers. Petrovic was tortured by Dimitrijević and his co-conspirators until he eventually revealed the location of the room's hidden door. The conspirators forced Milan and his wife to open the door, and greeted them with a murderous volley when they did so, continuing to discharge their weapons into their corpses after they had fallen to the ground.

Victory in the Balkans in territories over which Austria-Hungary was supposed to have significant influence emboldened the Serbian military and the even more aggressive Balkan nationalists, who began an aggressive anti-Austrian campaign. Serbia funded rabble-rousers to inflame revolt and dissatisfaction throughout Austria's southeastern territories, and in addition to this, the Serbian secret police also began funding, training and equipping "lone wolf" assassins living within the Austro-Hungarian borders and encouraging them to target officials of the Empire. Although this campaign was largely unsuccessful, it provided further diplomatic strains between the two countries.

A state of unease and tension continued to reign between Serbia and Austria-Hungary for the next few years. By the end of 1910 General Varesanin had crushed the Bosnian independence movement apparently for good. However, the situation was still tense as late as 1913, when Austrian Archduke Franz Ferdinand, in his newly established capacity as Inspector General of the Austro-Hungarian Armed Forces, was ordered by his uncle to visit Bosnia. There he was to inspect the military maneuvers of the Bosnian Army, before proceeding to Sarajevo, where he would preside with his wife over the opening of a new museum of the Bosnian state.

The tension in the Balkans, where by 1913 the Ottoman Empire's holdings had been reduced to the point of non-existence in the wake of Serbian, Bulgarian, Greek, Montenegrin and newly independent Albanian expansion, was symptomatic of what was occurring in Europe as a whole. By 1900 there existed in Europe an interconnected series of alliances, treaties and pacts, both overt and secret, that were intended to maintain the balance of power and the status quo on the mainland, the likes of which had never been seen before. The purpose of this web of alliances was ostensibly to ensure peace, but in reality it meant that an aggressive power could wage small-scale wars with virtual impunity thanks to the looming threat of a full-scale escalation on the European mainland, as had occurred during the Schleiswig-Holstein Question and the Franco-Prussian War (both conflicts started by what was now Germany).

The first of these alliances had emerged in the wake of the Napoleonic Wars with the creation of the Holy Alliance, a "triumvirate" of Austria, Russia and Prussia. 60 years later, Otto von Bismarck, perhaps the greatest politician of his age (and certainly the most effective champion of the Prussian cause), created the *dreikaiserbund*, the League of the Three Caesars, a re-affirmation of the previous alliance renegotiated to include Germany. Fittingly, this alliance fell apart over the Balkans, as Russia and Austria-Hungary were at odds over how to administer and exert influence across the region. Thus, in 1879, Germany and Austria-Hungary dropped Russia as a partner to form the Dual Alliance, and three years later, Austria set aside its differences with Italy, which had recently fought two viciously contested wars of independence against Austria to achieve sovereignty. Together, these three nations formed the Triple Alliance.

Bismarck

Things held together (albeit in an extremely fragile fashion) until roughly 1890, shortly after the ascension to the throne of Germany of Kaiser Wilhelm II. Wilhelm was concerned about the vast and shadowy power still wielded by Bismarck, so he compelled Bismarck to resign out of fear that he would undermine the legitimacy and power of the German monarchy by being the de facto ruler. This was a legitimate fear given that the diplomatic circles of Europe still contacted Bismarck over matters of international policy thanks to their decades-long familiarity with him. What Wilhelm failed to take into account was just how much Bismarck had wielded his personality, ruthlessness, personal magnetism and sheer diplomatic brilliance to keep Germany safe and ensure its constant expansion despite the minefield of European politics. With Bismarck gone, the fragile, informal diplomatic ties he had maintained disintegrated, and in 1890 the Kaiser committed a serious political blunder by refusing to renew the Re-Insurance Treaty, which guaranteed mutual non-aggression between Russia and Germany. Russia then went on to sign the Franco-Russian Alliance with France in 1902, effectively hemming in Germany between two largely hostile powers. France also signed a treaty with Britain, the Entente Cordiale, and in 1907 Britain involved itself further in European affairs by signing the Anglo-Russian Convention. These were not formal alliances, but for simplicity's sake, this complex Anglo-Russian-French arrangement is usually referred to as the Triple Entente. While there were no formal guarantees that Britain would intervene if either France or Russia were attacked or went to war, they certainly strengthened the possibility that this would occur.

Matters in Europe were further complicated by the massive escalation of an arms race. In the wake of the Franco-Prussian War of 1871, Germany had established itself as the dominant power in Europe, and German industrial output had grown by orders of magnitude. By the dawn of the 20th century, Germany was even competing with the mighty Royal Navy for domain over the world's oceans, an impressive output for a country that had never truly made naval power a priority. The *Kaiserliche Marine*, with its modern destroyers, worried the British so much that in 1906 they launched HMS *Dreadnought*, the most powerful battleship of its time. This race for technological supremacy was as much saber-rattling as it was a genuine policy to ensure sufficiently modern equipment in fear of an attack by another European great power, but regardless, military spending almost doubled among most of the powerful nations. Moreover, virtually all nations adopted new breech-loading bolt-action rifles to go along with new artillery pieces, heavy and super-heavy mortars and railway guns, machine guns, grenades, poison gas shells, and a host of other instruments of destruction.

As a result, weapons were becoming deadlier and more powerful just as nations like Germany and Italy were following burgeoning imperialistic agendas, and just as the British and French sought to prevent their expansion. The situation was incredibly volatile, and by 1914, all that was needed was a spark.

With Europe anticipating a potential war, all that was missing was a conflagration. The final straw came June 28, 1914, when a Serbian assassinated Archduke Franz Ferdinand, the heir to the throne of Austria-Hungary, in Sarajevo, Bosnia. Austria-Hungary immediately issued ultimatums to Serbia. When they declared war on Serbia July 28, 1914, Russia mobilized for war as well. The Germans mobilized in response to Russia on July 30, and the French, still smarting from the Franco-Prussian War, mobilized for war against Germany. The British also declared war on Germany on August 4. Thus, in the span of one week, six nations had declared war, half of which had no interest in the Balkans.

Though nobody can know for sure, it's altogether possible that World War I would have still broken out even if Franz Ferdinand had not been murdered. Regardless of events in the Balkans, Germany was already bellicose, France and Austria were concerned and involved, Russia was outwardly aggressive but also dealing with internal dissatisfaction, Italy was poised on the brink, and Britain was desperate to remain aloof but committed to its continental allies and a host of smaller countries clamoring for independence. Europe was too explosive to be rescued by any but the best of diplomats, if at all.

When World War I began in earnest, the Concert of Europe was clearly a thing of the past, though by this time, the Inter-Parliamentary Union had begun meeting in 1889. While it would also fail, the Inter-Parliamentary Union would provide direct inspiration for the League of Nations.

Chapter 2: We Must Bring About a League or a Union of Nations

"[I]n some form or other we must bring about a league or a union of nations with some common organ of consultation on all vital issues. … I would favour something more elastic, something more flexible, something which will be capable of adapting itself to the very complex circumstances which arise from time to time in our complex European relations, and it is perhaps possible in that way to achieve more real good. Now I would throw out a suggestion here that the time has come, especially now that America is also in this war, when more ample consideration should be given to the details of the subject. I know a great literature has already gathered round this subject of the common institutions, the common organs for a League of Nations. But I am sure the matter is more difficult than has been shown in any book that I have read on the subject, and I would throw out the suggestion that the time has come when an Anglo-American Committee- should be appointed to go thoroughly into it. …a great deal of consideration has been given to the subject in America. … I throw out this suggestion of an Anglo-American Committee as one that is worthy of consideration." - Jan Smuts, 1917

Jan Smuts

No matter what philosophical ideas came before, it was ultimately the carnage of World War I, and a growing understanding that man's ability to create weapons was outstripping his wisdom regarding when to use them, that set the stage for global attempts to create a peacekeeping organization. Put simply, had the European leaders understood just how catastrophic the war would be when it started in 1914, it doubtless would have been avoided.

During the war, several individuals put forth the idea that helped birth the League of Nations. Tellingly, they came from one rising world power, the United States, and one not yet aware of its declining stature, Great Britain. While it was ultimately President Woodrow Wilson who brought the organization into international prominence, Goldsworthy Lowes Dickinson and Lord Bryce of England first used the term "League of Nations" in 1914 when they created the League of Nations Union in that nation. In 1915, Dickinson wrote of his "League of Peace," "The improbability of war, I believe, would be increased in proportion as the issues of foreign policy should be known to and controlled by public opinion. There must be an end of the secret diplomacy which has plunged us into this catastrophe. To say this is not, of course, to suggest that complicated and delicate negotiations should be conducted in public. But there should be no more secret treaties or arrangements of any kind.... All nations ought to know and constantly be reminded of all their commitments to other Powers, and all the complications which constitute the danger centres of Europe. I am aware of all that may be said about the latent Jingoism of crowds, and the power of an unscrupulous press to work upon it. But we have all that as it is. It is what Governments rely upon and call upon when they intend to make war. The essence of the present situation is that no other forces have time to organize themselves, because we are actually at war before we have begun to realize the crisis. With plenty of time and full knowledge the better elements of public opinion could be rallied. The proposed League of Peace would secure the necessary delay. If, then, at the last, the public opinion of any nations insisted on war, there would be war. But at least every force working against war would have come into play."

Wilson

Dickinson

Lord Bryce

While England had the Bryce Group, the United States had the "League to Enforce Peace," led in part by former President William Taft. Like its British counterpart, this organization saw itself as a temporary entity, not as an ongoing concern. Meanwhile, it was the Fabian Society in England that came up with the idea of a permanent international court that would hear cases between opposing countries.

Taft

In 1918, Lord Balfour, then the British Foreign Secretary, tasked Lord Robert Cecil with creating the first official report on the possibility of creating a world peace organization. The Phillimore Commission, named for Walter Phillimore, its head, suggested that the nations create a "Conference of Allied States" to arbitrate disputes between countries. The British Parliament agreed to the plan, and the French also came up with their own proposal that included an "international army" that would be authorized to enforce decisions made by the international court.

Lord Balfour

Cecil

Phillimore

Conversely, some Europeans didn't understand the notion of creating treaties with other countries when it was precisely what helped instigate World War I in the first place. Maurice Hankey, the British Cabinet Secretary, wrote a memorandum heavily criticizing the notion of such a league: "Generally it appears to me that any such scheme is dangerous to us, because it will create a sense of security which is wholly fictitious…It [a League of Nations] will only result in failure and the longer that failure is postponed the more certain it is that this country will have been lulled to sleep. It will put a very strong lever into the hands of the well-meaning idealists who are to be found in almost every Government, who deprecate expenditure on armaments, and, in the course of time, it will almost certainly result in this country being caught at a disadvantage." A British foreign office minister, Sir Eyre Crowe, made a similar argument, writing that "a solemn league and covenant" would be "a treaty, like other treaties…What is there to ensure that it will not, like other treaties, be broken?"

Meanwhile, on the other side of the pond, President Wilson was also working to formulate plans for global cooperation and peace. Wilson's Fourteen Points sought to reassure Americans that the war was being fought for ideas, not to assuage the power of European monarchs. The points varied in their specificity, with some detailing concrete plans for post-war Europe, and others being statements of idealism.

    I.   Open covenants of peace, openly arrived at, after which there shall be no private international understandings of any kind but diplomacy shall proceed always frankly and in the public view.

    II.   Absolute freedom of navigation upon the seas, outside territorial waters, alike in peace and in war, except as the seas may be closed in whole or in part by international action for the enforcement of international covenants.

    III.   The removal, so far as possible, of all economic barriers and the establishment of an equality of trade conditions among all the nations consenting to the peace and associating themselves for its maintenance.

    IV.   Adequate guarantees given and taken that national armaments will be reduced to the lowest point consistent with domestic safety.

    V.   A free, open-minded, and absolutely impartial adjustment of all colonial claims, based upon a strict observance of the principle that in determining all such questions of sovereignty the interests of the populations concerned must have equal weight with the equitable claims of the government whose title is to be determined.

    VI.   The evacuation of all Russian territory and such a settlement of all questions affecting Russia as will secure the best and freest cooperation of the other nations of the world in obtaining for her an unhampered and unembarrassed opportunity for the independent determination of her own political development and national policy and assure her of a sincere welcome into the society of free nations under institutions of her own choosing; and, more than a welcome, assistance also of every kind that she may need and may herself desire. The treatment accorded Russia by her sister nations in the months to come will be the acid test of their good will, of their comprehension of her needs as distinguished from their own interests, and of their intelligent and unselfish sympathy.

VII. Belgium, the whole world will agree, must be evacuated and restored, without any attempt to limit the sovereignty which she enjoys in common with all other free nations. No other single act will serve as this will serve to restore confidence among the nations in the laws which they have themselves set and determined for the government of their relations with one another. Without this healing act the whole structure and validity of international law is forever impaired.

VIII. All French territory should be freed and the invaded portions restored, and the wrong done to France by Prussia in 1871 in the matter of Alsace-Lorraine, which has unsettled the peace of the world for nearly fifty years, should be righted, in order that peace may once more be made secure in the interest of all.

IX. A readjustment of the frontiers of Italy should be effected along clearly recognizable lines of nationality.

X. The peoples of Austria-Hungary, whose place among the nations we wish to see safeguarded and assured, should be accorded the freest opportunity to autonomous development.

XI. Rumania, Serbia, and Montenegro should be evacuated; occupied territories restored; Serbia accorded free and secure access to the sea; and the relations of the several Balkan states to one another determined by friendly counsel along historically established lines of allegiance and nationality; and international guarantees of the political and economic independence and territorial integrity of the several Balkan states should be entered into.

XII. The Turkish portion of the present Ottoman Empire should be assured a secure sovereignty, but the other nationalities which are now under Turkish rule should be assured an undoubted security of life and an absolutely unmolested opportunity of autonomous development, and the Dardanelles should be permanently opened as a free passage to the ships and commerce of all nations under international guarantees.

XIII. An independent Polish state should be erected which should include the territories inhabited by indisputably Polish populations, which should be assured a free and secure access to the sea, and whose political and economic independence and territorial integrity should be guaranteed by international covenant.

 XIV. A general association of nations must be formed under specific covenants for the purpose of affording mutual guarantees of political independence and territorial integrity to great and small states alike.

In delivering these points, Wilson articulated the aims of the war more comprehensively than any of his European counterparts, who often had trouble selling the war to their constituents. At the same time, despite his cogency, leaders in Britain and France were skeptical of Wilson's idealism. Many liked and respected it, but they thought it was unrealistic in practice. Many Americans, while rallying behind the President, felt the same. The final point was perhaps the most controversial, and establishing a "general association of nations" would soon prove harder than Wilson imagined.

In 1918 though, Jan Smuts of South Africa was pleased with Wilson's interest and felt American involvement was essential for success, though he also conceded, "America has been so far from the danger that she has built up an ideal in the clouds, whereas here in Europe we labour in the trough of the sea. America has got there too now, and if we could now bring together not only the idealists, but also practical men, men of experience, men who know the difficult ways of the world and the bad ways of the world if we could bring them together in a committee to thrash out a detailed scheme, it would be possible to have something more practical than anything we have yet seen on this subject, which might be invaluable when the time for peace negotiations arrives."

World War I was characterized by the stalemate of trench warfare for several years, but at 11:00 a.m. on the 11th day of the 11th month in 1918, the "war to end all wars" finally came to an end. The Armistice brought about the cessation of all offensive activities in Europe, and the points detailed in the text of the armistice itself were mainly decided by Marshal Ferdinand Foch, the Supreme Allied Commander. Though based upon Wilson's Fourteen Points, what they meant in brief was a complete and utter defeat for Germany. All military hostilities were to cease immediately within six hours, and Germany would withdraw all remaining troops from France, Luxembourg, Belgium and Alsace-Lorraine within two weeks. The Germans would also be obliged to pull back from their positions in Turkey, Romania and Austro-Hungary and resume the 1914 border line. Likewise, they would have to withdraw all forces on the Western front to the Rhine and submit to Allied occupation of a buffer zone. The German navy would also be confined to port, and all its submarines surrendered to the Allies, along with 5,000 artillery pieces, 25,000 machine guns, 3,000 mortars, 1,700 airplanes, 5,000 train locomotives and 150,000 train cars.

A painting depicting the signing of the Armistice in a carriage of Foch's private train, CIWL #2419

Foch (second from right in the front) at the signing of the Armistice

As the terms suggest, there was no sympathy for the Germans, either in the armistice terms or in those of the peace that followed. Likewise, public opinion (and that of the troops who had fought so hard and for so long) was strongly in favor of making examples out of the Germans. Millions had died, France and Belgium had been devastated, and Russia had been plunged into a bloody revolution, and it was firmly believed that the Germans had been responsible for all of it and thus deserved everything they got. Accordingly, the Allies kept firing upon the German positions right until the very last possible second before the armistice came into effect. Carting spare ammunition back to the artillery depots seemed like an unnecessary task when it could simply be fired at the Germans, particularly in case they decided not to honor the terms of the agreement. In fact, Allied artillery was responsible for over 10,000 casualties on November 11th alone, with what was likely the final shot of the war being fired by Battery 4 of the U.S. Navy's Railway Guns at 10:57:30.

What followed World War I in the shell-shocked vacuum of a war-ravaged Germany is well-known, and the merits of meting out such a ruthless punishment on the losers, and the resentment and hatred this fostered within the German population, has been debated at length. That said, it is difficult not to sympathize with the decision-makers who forced the terms of surrender down the Kaiser's throat after seeing millions of their young men march off to fight and die against what they saw as unrepentant German aggression. The peace process was always bound to be an emotional issue, particularly for the French and Belgians at the table who had seen huge swaths of their countries turned into barren, shell-blasted wastelands by four years of warfare.

Nonetheless, some of the veterans at the time presumed the Great War would not be the "war to end all wars." Indeed, Foch himself prophetically asserted, "This is not a peace. It is an armistice for 20 years," and indeed, less than 22 years later, another Armistice would be signed in the same railway carriage used in November 1918, but this time, it would bring about the end of hostilities in France after the Germans were victorious. A memorial building housing the carriage had been erected in 1927, and Adolf Hitler would symbolically use it for the surrender of France in 1940. American journalist William Shirer wrote of Hitler's reaction at the sight of the memorial and the carriage: "Through my glasses I saw the Führer stop, glance at the [Alsace-Lorraine] monument.... Then he read the inscription on the great granite block in the center of the clearing: 'Here on the eleventh of November 1918 succumbed the criminal pride of the German empire...vanquished by the free peoples which it tried to enslave.' I look for the expression on Hitler's face. I am but fifty yards from him and see him through my glasses as though he were directly in front of me. I have seen that face many times at the great moments of his life. But today! It is afire with scorn, anger, hate, revenge, triumph. He steps off the monument and contrives to make even this gesture a masterpiece of contempt. He glances back at it contemptuous, angry...Suddenly, as though his face were not giving quite complete expression to his feelings, he throws his whole body into harmony with his mood. He swiftly snaps his hands on his hips, arches his shoulders, plants his feet wide apart. It is a magnificent gesture of defiance, of burning contempt..." After that Armistice was signed, the building was destroyed and the carriage was brought back to Berlin. It would take almost 5 more years for the Nazis to be decisively defeated, and as the Allies pushed towards Berlin at the end of World War II, the SS put the carriage to the torch.

Chapter 3: There Must Be a Union Which Has Force Behind It

"There remains another condition...that in any arrangement for future peace there should be at the back of it some sanction, some force otherwise it remains merely talk, otherwise it remains simply a vision. A nation which has got off the rails, or intends to get off the rails, must know that in the last resort the League of Nations against her are going to use force, and are going to force her on the right rails if she is not going willingly to come back. It is not merely sufficient for a conference to meet from time to time like an Areopagus to discuss questions, but there must be a union which has force behind it and which is bound to use that force when the occasion arises. What force has to be used, and in what form or measure it is to be used, that, of course, is a very difficult question. You know the plan this Society and also the American Society favours is of a more limited character, and would apply force not to prevent war, but to ensure consultation; to ensure inquiry and to afford a certain time for consideration and inquiry and for a decision to be arrived at." - Jan Smuts

"I can predict with absolute certainty that within another generation there will be another world war if the nations of the world do not concert the method by which to prevent it." - Wilson

During the Paris Peace Conference that officially ended World War I in 1919, Wilson, Smuts and Cecil all showed up with their own version of the covenant for the League of Nations. The three versions were considered, debated and adjusted to create the final covenant on January 25, and six months later, on June 28, 1919, the covenant officially became Part 1 of the Treaty of Versailles. It began, "In order to promote international co-operation and to achieve international peace and security by the acceptance of obligations not to resort to war, by the prescription of open, just and honourable relations between nations, by the firm establishment of the understandings of international law as the actual rule of conduct among Governments, and by the maintenance of justice and a scrupulous respect for all treaty obligations in the dealings of organized peoples with one another....."

In addition to outlining how the League would be organized, the covenant also set guidelines for how the member countries would behave themselves: "The Members of the League recognise that the maintenance of peace requires the reduction of national armaments to the lowest point consistent with national safety and the enforcement by common action of international obligations. The Council, taking account of the geographical situation and circumstances of each State, shall formulate plans for such reduction for the consideration and action of the several Governments. Such plans shall be subject to reconsideration and revision at least every ten years. After these plans shall have been adopted by the several Governments, the limits of armaments therein fixed shall not be exceeded without the concurrence of the Council. The Members of the League agree that the manufacture by private enterprise of munitions and implements of war is open to grave objections. The Council shall advise how the evil effects attendant upon such manufacture can be prevented, due regard being had to the necessities of those Members of the League which are not able to manufacture the munitions and implements of war necessary for their safety. The Members of the League undertake to interchange full and frank information as to the scale of their armaments, their military, naval and air programmes and the condition of such of their industries as are adaptable to war-like purposes."

The armament clause was a difficult one, with even Smuts admitting, "It is no use trying to prevent war when nations are armed to the teeth. If Governments are allowed with impunity to prepare for war over a long process of years, to consolidate all their resources on a military basis with a view to making an attack…then inevitably you reach a point when not even a League of Nations is sufficiently strong to withstand the deluge. And however difficult and it is a most difficult subject when it is thoroughly gone into it seems to me that this matter also will have to be dealt with in some form or another and in some degree or another namely, the devising of plans which will lead to the abolition or diminution of armaments and to less recourse being had by States to warlike preparations in future."

All this sounded nice, of course, but the question of how the league could actually prevent war from breaking out remained. Articles 10-12 dealt with this issue specifically, and Article 10 would turn out to be the most controversial: "The Members of the League undertake to respect and preserve as against external aggression the territorial integrity and existing political independence of all Members of the League. In case of any such aggression or in case of any threat or danger of such aggression the Council shall advise upon the means by which this obligation shall be fulfilled."

This article would prove the most difficult for Wilson to sell to the American people, who were still stinging from the lives lost in what was widely viewed as a European war. Moreover, Articles 11 and 12 did nothing to allay anyone's fears:

"ARTICLE 11.

"Any war or threat of war, whether immediately affecting any of the Members of the League or not, is hereby declared a matter of concern to the whole League, and the League shall take any action that may be deemed wise and effectual to safeguard the peace of nations. In case any such emergency should arise the Secretary General shall on the request of any Member of the League forthwith summon a meeting of the Council. It is also declared to be the friendly right of each Member of the League to bring to the attention of the Assembly or of the Council any circumstance whatever affecting international relations which threatens to disturb international peace or the good understanding between nations upon which peace depends.

"ARTICLE 12.

"The Members of the League agree that, if there should arise between them any dispute likely to lead to a rupture they will submit the matter either to arbitration or judicial settlement or to enquiry by the Council, and they agree in no case to resort to war until three months after the award by the arbitrators or the judicial decision, or the report by the Council. In any case under this Article the award of the arbitrators or the judicial decision shall be made within a reasonable time, and the report of the Council shall be made within six months after the submission of the dispute."

Since it was asking member countries not to go to war with each other, the League needed to offer them some other way of solving their disputes. It did so in Article 13:

"The Members of the League agree that whenever any dispute shall arise between them which they recognise to be suitable for submission to arbitration or judicial settlement and which cannot be satisfactorily settled by diplomacy, they will submit the whole subject-matter to arbitration or judicial settlement.

"Disputes as to the interpretation of a treaty, as to any question of international law, as to the existence of any fact which if established would constitute a breach of any international obligation, or as to the extent and nature of the reparation to be made for any such breach, are declared to be among those which are generally suitable for submission to arbitration or judicial settlement.

"For the consideration of any such dispute, the court to which the case is referred shall be the Permanent Court of International Justice, established in accordance with Article 14, or any tribunal agreed on by the parties to the dispute or stipulated in any convention existing between them.

"The Members of the League agree that they will carry out in full good faith any award or decision that may be rendered, and that they will not resort to war against a Member of the League which complies therewith. In the event of any failure to carry out such an award or decision, the Council shall propose what steps should be taken to give effect thereto."

For an organization aiming to avoid war, the new League needed to come up with a way for nations to solve their conflicts. The creators of the League of Nations knew this and soon turned their attention to coming up with effective alternatives to armed battles via Article 14:

"The Council shall formulate and submit to the Members of the League for adoption plans for the establishment of a Permanent Court of International Justice. The Court shall be competent to hear and determine any dispute of an international character which the parties thereto submit to it. The Court may also give an advisory opinion upon any dispute or question referred to it by the Council or by the Assembly." Then they went on to get more specific, saying Article 15:

"If there should arise between Members of the League any dispute likely to lead to a rupture, which is not submitted to arbitration or judicial settlement in accordance with Article 13, the Members of the League agree that they will submit the matter to the Council. Any party to the dispute may effect such submission by giving notice of the existence of the dispute to the Secretary General, who will make all necessary arrangements for a full investigation and consideration thereof. For this purpose the parties to the dispute will communicate to the Secretary General, as promptly as possible, statements of their case with all the relevant facts and papers, and the Council may forthwith direct the publication thereof. The Council shall endeavour to effect a settlement of the dispute, and if such efforts are successful, a statement shall be made public giving such facts and explanations regarding the dispute and the terms of settlement thereof as the Council may deem appropriate. If the dispute is not thus settled, the Council either unanimously or by a majority vote shall make and publish a report containing a statement of the facts of the dispute and the recommendations which are deemed just and proper in regard thereto. Any Member of the League represented on the Council may make public a statement of the facts of the dispute and of its conclusions regarding the same. If a report by the Council is unanimously agreed to by the members thereof other than the Representatives of one or more of the parties to the dispute, the Members of the League agree that they will not go to war with any party to the dispute which complies with the recommendations of the report."

What, then, was to be done if the Council itself could not determine what the right thing to do was? The answer was far from clear, since it was designed to at the same time be attractive and forceful. Nevertheless, the writers tried with this passage: "If the Council fails to reach a report which is unanimously agreed to by the members thereof, other than the Representatives of one or more of the parties to the dispute, the Members of the League reserve to themselves the right to take such action as they shall consider necessary for the maintenance of right and justice. If the dispute between the parties is claimed by one of them, and is found by the Council, to arise out of a matter which by international law is solely within the domestic jurisdiction of that party, the Council shall so report, and shall make no recommendation as to its settlement. The Council may in any case under this Article refer the dispute to the Assembly. The dispute shall be so referred at the request of either party to the dispute, provided that such request be made within fourteen days after the submission of the dispute to the Council. In any case referred to the Assembly, all the provisions of this Article and of Article 12 relating to the action and powers of the Council shall apply to the action and powers of the Assembly, provided that a report made by the Assembly, if concurred in by the Representatives of those Members of the League represented on the Council and of a majority of the other Members of the League, exclusive in each case of the Representatives of the parties to the dispute, shall have the same force as a report by the Council concurred in by all the members thereof other than the Representatives of one or more of the parties to the dispute."

In Article 16, it was time to answer the ultimate question: would the League of Nations go to war to prevent war? Smuts himself asked this, musing in 1917, "Ought nations to go to war at once if it is necessary to keep the peace, or should they go in for a more limited application of force, like a. financial boycott or a blockade of communications, or a pacific blockade or something of the kind? These are all questions of the greatest difficulty which might be threshed out carefully...."

Though the drafters of these articles didn't know it at the time, this was the League's fatal flaw, because the member nations would essentially watch Nazi Germany, a fellow member of the League of Nations, build up a military and navy in ways that violated the Treaty of Versailles. While the Allies would be castigated for their appeasement strategy, there was no effective way to use the League of Nations because of the following passage: "Should any Member of the League resort to war in disregard of its covenants under Articles 12, 13 or 15, it shall ipso facto be deemed to have committed an act of war against all other Members of the League, which hereby undertake immediately to subject it to the severance of all trade or financial relations, the prohibition of all intercourse between their nationals and the nationals of the covenant-breaking State, and the prevention of all financial, commercial or personal intercourse between the nationals of the covenant-breaking State and the nationals of any other State, whether a Member of the League or not. It shall be the duty of the Council in such case to recommend to the several Governments concerned what effective military, naval or air force the Members of the League shall severally contribute to the armed forces to be used to protect the covenants of the League. The Members of the League agree, further, that they will mutually support one another in the financial and economic measures which are taken under this Article, in order to minimise the loss and inconvenience resulting from the above measures, and that they will mutually support one another in resisting any special measures aimed at one of their number by the covenant-breaking State, and that they will take the necessary steps to afford passage through their territory to the forces of any of the Members of the League which are co-operating to protect the covenants of the League. Any Member of the League which has violated any covenant of the League may be declared to be no longer a Member of the League by a vote of the Council concurred in by the Representatives of all the other Members of the League represented thereon."

While the League had a plan for dealing with disputes between member nations peacefully, it also had to face the reality that not every nation of the world would join the organization, and that controversies would develop between member nations and other countries. The charter addressed this potential issue in Article 17: "In the event of a dispute between a Member of the League and a State which is not a Member of the League, or between States not Members of the League, the State or States not Members of the League shall be invited to accept the obligations of membership in the League for the purposes of such dispute, upon such conditions as the Council may deem just. If such invitation is accepted, the provisions of Articles 12 to 16 inclusive shall be applied with such modifications as may be deemed necessary by the Council.

Upon such invitation being given the Council shall immediately institute an inquiry into the circumstances of the dispute and recommend such action as may seem best and most effectual in the circumstances. If a State so invited shall refuse to accept the obligations of membership in the League for the purposes of such dispute, and shall resort to war against a Member of the League, the provisions of Article 16 shall be applicable as against the State taking such action. If both parties to the dispute when so invited refuse to accept the obligations of membership in the League for the purposes of such dispute, the Council may take such measures and make such recommendations as will prevent hostilities and will result in the settlement of the dispute."

Like a parent with a large family, the League of Nations needed some way to keep two or three nations from "ganging up" on the other members. This was tricky, since it spoke directly to the policy-making activities of sovereign governments. Nonetheless, Articles 18-21 attempted to address this:

"ARTICLE 18.

"Every treaty or international engagement entered into hereafter by any Member of the League shall be forthwith registered with the Secretariat and shall as soon as possible be published by it. No such treaty or international engagement shall be binding until so registered." Articles 19 and 20 went even further, though Article 21 softened the blow:

"ARTICLE 19.

"The Assembly may from time to time advise the reconsideration by Members of the League of treaties which have become inapplicable and the consideration of international conditions whose continuance might endanger the peace of the world.

"ARTICLE 20.

"The Members of the League severally agree that this Covenant is accepted as abrogating all obligations or understandings inter se which are inconsistent with the terms thereof, and solemnly undertake that they will not hereafter enter into any engagements inconsistent with the terms thereof.

"In case any Member of the League shall, before becoming a Member of the League, have undertaken any obligations inconsistent with the terms of this Covenant, it shall be the duty of such Member to take immediate steps to procure its release from such obligations.

"ARTICLE 21.

"Nothing in this Covenant shall be deemed to affect the validity of international engagements, such as treaties of arbitration or regional understandings like the Monroe doctrine, for securing the maintenance of peace."

Since the League was founded at the end of what was at that point the deadliest war in human history, it was understandably concerned with how to deal with colonies that had been destroyed and often disowned by the nations that had colonized them. Though many European countries hadn't yet accepted it, the sun was setting on the era of European imperialism, and founders of the League felt a responsibility to help those colonies that were becoming independent make their way into full nation-states.

Over time, these efforts would be among the most controversial of the League's short lifetime. For instance, Article 22 established, "To those colonies and territories which as a consequence of the late war have ceased to be under the sovereignty of the States which formerly governed them and which are inhabited by peoples not yet able to stand by themselves under the strenuous conditions of the modern world, there should be applied the principle that the well-being and development of such peoples form a sacred trust of civilisation and that securities for the performance of this trust should be embodied in this Covenant."

This was a noble idea, but the League would ultimately be made up of men, not angels, and those developing the covenant knew that there had to be some policy put in place to protect the indigenous peoples from even the best-intentions of foreign leaders. Thus, the article declared, "The best method of giving practical effect to this principle is that the tutelage of such peoples should be entrusted to advanced nations who by reason of their resources, their experience or their geographical position can best undertake this responsibility, and who are willing to accept it, and that this tutelage should be exercised by them as Mandatories on behalf of the League. The character of the mandate must differ according to the stage of the development of the people, the geographical situation of the territory, its economic conditions, and other similar circumstances."

The policy would be, then, that any nation seeking to assist another smaller country would do so not for its own benefit but under the supervision of the League.

At this point, Article 22 made specific references that were somewhat out of keeping with what was supposed to be the eternal nature of the covenant. It began by saying, "Certain communities formerly belonging to the Turkish Empire have reached a stage of development where their existence as independent nations can be provisionally recognised subject to the rendering of administrative advice and assistance by a Mandatory until such time as they are able to stand alone. The wishes of these communities must be a principal consideration in the selection of the Mandatory." This group was later designated "A."

This suggestion was all well and good, but it drew attention to one of the problems with the covenant itself: those writing it were approaching the problems of the entire world from a very

Anglo-centric worldview. Though their decisions would have ramifications in places like the Middle East for the next 100 years, many of them detrimental, the drafters felt completely comfortable deciding who was ready for independence and who was not: "Other peoples, especially those of Central Africa, are at such a stage that the Mandatory must be responsible for the administration of the territory under conditions which will guarantee freedom of conscience and religion, subject only to the maintenance of public order and morals, the prohibition of abuses such as the slave trade, the arms traffic, and the liquor traffic, and the prevention of the establishment of fortifications or military and naval bases and of military training of the natives for other than police purposes and the defence of territory, and will also secure equal opportunities for the trade and commerce of other Members of the League." This group was designated "B."

The League also designated another group as "C." "There are territories, such as South-West Africa and certain of the South Pacific Islands, which, owing to the sparseness of their population, or their small size, or their remoteness from the centres of civilisation, or their geographical contiguity to the territory of the Mandatory, and other circumstances, can be best administered under the laws of the Mandatory as integral portions of its territory, subject to the safeguards above mentioned in the interests of the indigenous population."

Given that so much territory would be administered as Mandates, the articles had to explain just what the Mandatory power would do. While this article was unusually specific about who it would be managing, it was just as open-ended about how they would manage: "In every case of mandate, the Mandatory shall render to the Council an annual report in reference to the territory committed to its charge. The degree of authority, control, or administration to be exercised by the Mandatory shall, if not previously agreed upon by the Members of the League, be explicitly defined in each case by the Council. A permanent Commission shall be constituted to receive and examine the annual reports of the Mandatories and to advise the Council on all matters relating to the observance of the mandates."

Not surprisingly, the victorious Allied powers took charge of creating the Mandate system, beginning on January 30, 1919. There were 14 mandatory territories, and their supervision was divided up among France, the United Kingdom, Belgium, the Union of South Africa, New Zealand, Japan and Australia. Only one territory, the Kingdom of Iraq, had its independence recognized during the League's lifetime.

Having dealt with issues of international importance, the agreement next focused on how the League would deal with domestic issues within its member states. Article 23 was indeed controversial, for it took the work of the League past the task of preventing war, something most people could agree was a good idea, and into the realm of how individual countries would treat their own citizens.

"Subject to and in accordance with the provisions of international conventions existing or hereafter to be agreed upon, the Members of the League:

"(a) will endeavour to secure and maintain fair and humane conditions of labour for men, women, and children, both in their own countries and in all countries to which their commercial and industrial relations extend, and for that purpose will establish and maintain the necessary international organisations;

"(b) undertake to secure just treatment of the native inhabitants of territories under their control;

"(c) will entrust the League with the general supervision over the execution of agreements with regard to the traffic in women and children, and the traffic in opium and other dangerous drugs;

"(d) will entrust the League with the general supervision of the trade in arms and ammunition with the countries in which the control of this traffic is necessary in the common interest;

"(e) will make provision to secure and maintain freedom of communications and of transit and equitable treatment for the commerce of all Members of the League. In this connection, the special necessities of the regions devastated during the war of 1914-1918 shall be borne in mind;

"(f) will endeavour to take steps in matters of international concern for the prevention and control of disease."

Article 25 added, "The Members of the League agree to encourage and promote the establishment and co-operation of duly authorised voluntary national Red Cross organisations having as purposes the improvement of health, the prevention of disease and the mitigation of suffering throughout the world."

There were two other articles that dealt with organization and ratification, but they were largely boilerplate in nature. The proposal for the League was complete and waited only for the response and, its writers hoped, ratification.

Photo of the members of the commission of the League of Nations created by the Plenary Session of the Preliminary Peace Conference, Paris, France, 1919. From *Le Pays de France* magazine

Chapter 4: A Practical Necessity

"A league of free nations had become a practical necessity. Examine the treaty of peace and you will find that everywhere throughout its manifold provisions its framers have felt obliged to turn to the League of Nations as an indispensable instrumentality for the maintenance of the new order it has been their purpose to set up in the world,—the world of civilized men. That there should be a league of nations to steady the counsels and maintain the peaceful understandings of the world, to make, not treaties alone, but the accepted principles of international law as well, the actual rule of conduct among the governments of the world, had been one of the agreements accepted from the first as the basis of peace with the Central Powers. The statesmen of all the belligerent countries were agreed that such a league must be created to sustain the settlements that were to be effected. But at first I think there was a feeling among some of them that, while it must be attempted, the formation of such a league was perhaps a counsel of perfection which practical men, long experienced in the world of affairs, must agree to very cautiously and with many misgivings. It was only as the difficult work of arranging an all-but-universal adjustment of the world's affairs advanced from day to day from one stage of conference to another that it became evident to them that what they were seeking would be little more than something written upon paper, to be interpreted and applied by such methods as the chances of politics might make available if they did not provide a means of common counsel which all were obliged to accept, a common authority whose decisions would be recognized as decisions that all must respect." - President Wilson

On July 10, 1919, Wilson went before the United States Senate to speak about the recently signed Treaty of Versailles. In his remarks, he lobbied for the creation of such an organization, asserting, "And so the most practical, the most skeptical among them turned more and more to the League as the authority through which international action was to be secured, the authority without which, as they had come to see it, it would be difficult to give assured effect either to this treaty or to any other international understanding upon which they were to depend for the maintenance of peace. The fact that the Covenant of the League was the first substantive part of the treaty to be worked out and agreed upon, while all else was in solution, helped to make the formulation of the rest easier. The Conference was, after all, not to be ephemeral. The concert of nations was to continue, under a definite Covenant which had been agreed upon and which all were convinced was workable. They could go forward with confidence to make arrangements intended to be permanent. The most practical of the conferees were at last the most ready to refer to the League of Nations the superintendence of all interests which did not admit of immediate determination, of all administrative problems which were to require a continuing oversight. What had seemed a counsel of perfection had come to seem a plain counsel of necessity. The League of Nations was the practical statesman's hope of success in many of the most difficult things he was attempting."

Wilson sacrificed his health and likely many years of his shortened life on behalf of the League, but he faced stiff opposition. On August 12, the powerful Republican Senator Henry Cabot Lodge responded to Wilson's plea for the League by retorting, "The independence of the United States is not only more precious to ourselves but to the world than any single possession…[I]n making this treaty and taking on these obligations all that we do is in a spirit of unselfishness and in a desire for the good of mankind. But it is well to remember that we are dealing with nations every one of which has a direct individual interest to serve, and there is grave danger in an unshared idealism. … I have always loved one flag and I cannot share that devotion [with] a mongrel banner created for a League. … The United States is the world's best hope, but if you fetter her in the interests and quarrels of other nations, if you tangle her in the intrigues of Europe, you will destroy her power for good and endanger her very existence. Leave her to march freely through the centuries to come as in the years that have gone. Strong, generous, and confident, she has nobly served mankind. Beware how you trifle with your marvellous inheritance, this great land of ordered liberty, for if we stumble and fall freedom and civilization everywhere will go down in ruin. We are told that we shall 'break the heart of the world' if we do not take this league just as it stands. I fear that the hearts of the vast majority of mankind would beat on strongly and steadily and without any quickening if the league were to perish altogether."

Henry Cabot Lodge

Having made clear his feelings on the matter, Lodge continued to explain why he felt so strongly about the issue: "We hear much of visions and I trust we shall continue to have visions and dream dreams of a fairer future for the race. But visions are one thing and visionaries are another, and the mechanical appliances of the rhetorician designed to give a picture of a present which does not exist and of a future which no man can predict are as unreal and short-lived as the steam or canvas clouds, the angels suspended on wires and the artificial lights of the stage. Ideals have been thrust upon us as an argument for the league until the healthy mind which rejects cant revolts from them. Are ideals confined to this deformed experiment upon a noble purpose, tainted, as it is, with bargains and tied to a peace treaty which might have been disposed of long ago to the great benefit of the world if it had not been compelled to carry this rider on its back? 'Post equitem sedet atra cura,' Horace tells us, but no blacker care ever sat behind any rider than we shall find in this covenant of doubtful and disputed interpretation as it now perches upon the treaty of peace."

To his credit, Lodge knew that most of those working for the League had good intentions at heart; he did not so much question their intentions as their methods: "No doubt many excellent and patriotic people see a coming fulfilment of noble ideals in the words 'league for peace.' We all respect and share these aspirations and desires, but some of us see no hope, but rather defeat, for them in this murky covenant. For we, too, have our ideals, even if we differ from those who have tried to establish a monopoly of idealism. Our first ideal is our country, and we see her in the future, as in the past, giving service to all her people and to the world. Our ideal of the future is that she should continue to render that service of her own free will. She has great problems of her own to solve, very grim and perilous problems, and a right solution, if we can attain to it, would largely benefit mankind. We would have our country strong to resist a peril from the West, as she has flung back the German menace from the East. We would not have our politics distracted and embittered by the dissensions of other lands. We would not have our country's vigour exhausted or her moral force abated, by everlasting meddling and muddling in every quarrel, great and small, which afflicts the world. Our ideal is to make her ever stronger and better and finer, because in that way alone, as we believe, can she be of the greatest service to the world's peace and to the welfare of mankind."

With his agenda seemingly spiraling out of control, Wilson figured that if Americans weren't buying the League of Nations, he'd try to sell it better. Wilson thus embarked on a public speaking tour that was almost immediately marred by poor health, including what was believed to be the flu in early 1919. The illness was attributed to the strains of his schedule, but the most serious blow would come starting that September, when Wilson suffered a couple of devastating strokes that left him paralyzed on one side. The physical ailments were bad enough, but the effects of the stroke altered his personality, making him combative and hostile. Those personal traits didn't exactly augment his ability to convince the Senate to ratify a treaty, and it was exacerbated by the fact that Wilson didn't seem to acknowledge or understand his new limitations.

The extent to which Wilson's personality even mattered at that point is still a mystery, because the exact nature of the presidency in 1920 is among the most controversial topics in presidential history. The full extent of Wilson's debilitating strokes and his incapacitation went unreported and was all but unknown even among the Cabinet members of the Wilson Administration. After his strokes, Wilson was confined to bed for several weeks, and his doctor and new wife Edith kept him away from just about everyone for the ostensible purpose of letting him recover. He could later use a wheelchair and eventually walk with a cane, but as his attitude change suggested, the strokes had impeded some of his mental faculties.

The complete extent of Wilson's incapacity remains unclear, as does the exact role his wife Edith played during the last year of his presidency. Edith took control of Wilson's schedule, and by serving as gatekeeper she essentially determined what issues came across Wilson's desk and which ones went to other officials in the executive branch. Of course, if President Wilson was incompetent, it means Edith was also probably making presidential decisions. And Edith went so far as to collaborate with chief of staff Joseph Patrick Tumulty to fashion a fake interview of the president supposedly conducted by journalist Louis Seibold. In 2008, author David Pietrusza published the aptly titled book *1920: The Year of the Six Presidents*. In the 1960s, the federal government would cite Wilson's incapacitation as the impetus for pushing through the 25th Amendment, which dealt with the presidential succession and empowered the Vice President when the president was incapacitated.

A June 1920 posed photograph of Wilson signing a document while Edith holds it steady for him.

Despite the unclear nature of the presidency that year, as the election of 1920 approach, Wilson became increasingly delusional. He thought he could achieve reelection to a third term, arguing that he was the only person willing to argue in favor of the League. Advisors to the President didn't have the heart to tell him his dreams were grossly unrealistic, and eventually the Democratic Party quashed any hope of a third term for Wilson. In that election, the referendum was largely on Wilson, despite his not being on the ballot, and Republican Warren G. Harding won the Presidency.

Wilson thus left the White House without the Senate having ratified the Treaty of Versailles, and the U.S. never joined Wilson's beloved League of Nations, to the consternation of other members.

THE GAP IN THE BRIDGE.

A political cartoon bemoaning America's absence in the League

An American cartoon critical of Wilson's League of Nations proposal with the following caption: President Wilson. "HERE'S YOUR OLIVE BRANCH. NOW GET BUSY." Dove of Peace. "OF COURSE I WANT TO PLEASE EVERYBODY; BUT ISN'T THIS A BIT THICK?"

Chapter 5: No Right To Run Away From Its Obligations

"'When we talk about, interest,' [Mr. Thomas] said 'we do not mean the exclusion of either Germany or Russia. When we talk of the League of Nations we want it to be a League of

Nations; that is to say, a League of all Nations.' Mr. Lloyd George replied: 'That is to say, if they want to Join it. Up to the present they have both refused to join. The Germans know perfectly well that if they apply we will support them. We will give them support not merely in the sense that they should be a member of the League, but that they should be on its Council. As for Russia, I know what M. Tchitherin says about the League of Nations. ' Replying to Mr. Thomas' remark that Labour believed the League of Nations was the instrument that ought to render the danger of war considerably less and that Labour equally believed there was a graver danger by the big States remaining out of it, Mr. Lloyd George said: ' I quite agree with you and I would include America.' 'And so would we ' said Mr. Thorn as. 'We think America who contributed to the Versailles treaty and its difficulties, has no right to run away from its obligations." - *The Gleaner*, October 18, 1922

In the end, the dreaded Article 10 kept the United States from joining 44 other countries across the world in joining and establishing the League of Nations, but the group met for the first time as a General Assembly on January 16, 1920. It was governed by an Executive Committee made up of the most powerful nation members, notably England and France. On November 1, the group moved from its temporary headquarters in London to Geneva, and it officially opened a few weeks later on November 20.

The official opening of the League of Nations on November 15, 1920

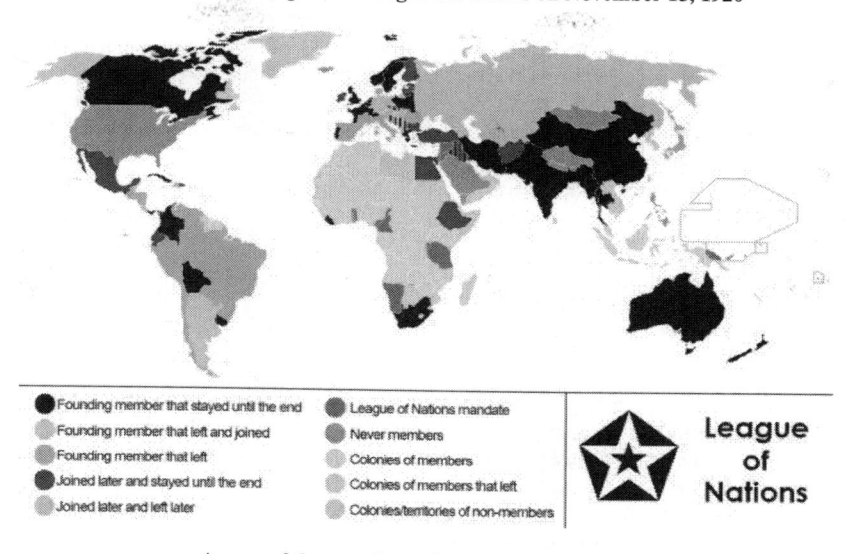

A map of the members of the League of Nations

Legend:
- Founding member that stayed until the end
- Founding member that left and joined
- Founding member that left
- Joined later and stayed until the end
- Joined later and left later
- League of Nations mandate
- Never members
- Colonies of members
- Colonies of members that left
- Colonies/territories of non-members

League of Nations

Over the years, the League of Nations grew to a maximum of 58 members in 1934, the same year the Soviet Union took its place among the ranks, and by then, the League had weathered a number of diplomatic storms, beginning with the one surrounding the Aland Islands, a large group of tiny islands located in the Baltic Sea. Lying about halfway between Sweden and Finland, they were taken over by Russia in 1809, the same year it annexed the eastern third of Sweden and established the Duchy of Finland. However, following Russia's Bolshevik Revolution, both nations were able to escape Russian domination; Finland declared itself once more a free nation and considered the Alands part of its country, but the Aland people wished to be part of Sweden. England asked the League to intervene, but Finland refused to be governed by the body, insisting that the matter was internal, not international. The League formed a commission on the issue anyway, and on June 24, 1921, it awarded the islands to Finland. The *Associated Press* reported, "The council of the League of Nations awarded the Aland islands in the Baltic sea to Finland The council decided that the islands should be neutralized from the military standpoint and the population given the guarantees recommended in the report of the commission of which Abram I. Leckus, of the United States was a member. Hjalmar Branting, of Sweden, protested against the decision but agreed to recognize it." As the newspaper article indicated, though the United States was never a member of the League, individual Americans did serve the organization in various capacities.

While dealing with the disagreement between Finland and Sweden, the League also had to mediate a dispute over Upper Silesia, a small country that had broken off from Poland after the war. The Treaty of Versailles had suggested it be made part of either Poland or Germany, and on May 20, 1921, a plebiscite was held in the country to allow its citizens to determine their nation's future. James Powers, writing for the *Boston Globe*, explained, "An election of nationalities is in progress today in a little by-corner of Central Europe— Silesia, That election will determine whether the people wish to belong to Poland or Germany...providing the decision meets with the approval of the Supreme Council of the Allies. It will also determine whether France will control practically all of the output of the German coal mines, for France is the hanker standing behind Poland. And, unless all indications during the past two months are amiss, tomorrow you will read in your paper an estimate of the casualties incident to the exercise of the franchise in! Silesia, and other results of the scramble which both Poland and Germany have been indulging in since the plans for the voting today began to mature."

At the same time, Herr Schroeder, the leader of the German Plebiscite Commission, insisted, "If Silesia goes Polish, it means her industrial ruin. If it goes to Germany, it makes the difference to Germany between barely existing and prosperity." C. A. Randau, of the American Polish Chamber of Commerce in the United States, took the opposite view, saying, "Poland bases her claim to Silesia on economic and racial grounds. To Germany the region means largely a source of greater wealth, whereas to Poland it is essential to economic independence. Germany received only 8.9 percent of her pre-war coal from Silesia while Poland got over 40 percent of her supply from Silesia. She has more than 60 percent of the population. She must win. To lose would be a calamity."

Violence did indeed break out after 60% of the Silesian voters chose to join Germany. With the Aland situation now handled, the League on August 12 created a commission to determine what should be done to end the violence and give the Silesians maximum control over their destinies. In the end, the League brokered an agreement in which Germany would take possession of most of Silesia's land but Poland would have control of the most developed parts of the area, particularly the parts with the most mineral wealth.

The League next dealt with settling the borders of Albania, a task left for it by the Paris Peace Conference of 1919. Greece and Yugoslavia both had troops in the area and there had been a number of skirmishes. In November 1921, the League agreed to leave the Albanian borders much as they had been in 1913, but conflict arose again when, on August 24, 1923, a group of Italians sent to mark out the border were killed. A week later, Italy's angry leader, Benito Mussolini, sent an Italian warship into the area to occupy the Greek island of Corfu. In the end, the League ordered Greek to pay reparations to Italy and Mussolini withdrew his men.

Even as the League conducted business over the years, the issue of whether to join it was repeatedly discussed in the United States. Those in favor of the League insisted that Americans needed to press their leaders to join, while those against it continued to claim that the nation was better off without it. As the situation in Albania heated up, a member of the latter group observed, "The European crisis precipitated by the trouble between Italy and Greece has been the occasion of increased activity on the part of League of Nations advocates in the United States. The burden of their propaganda now is to the effect that if the United States had been in the league the Italian-Grecian trouble would not have arisen; and if we were in the league now the league would be able to make these two nations speedily come to peaceful adjustment of their differences. The test of such propaganda is a statement of facts. The kingdom of Albania was dismembered over its protest by the European powers at Paris. After the League of Nations was formed the Albanians appealed to that body posed of representatives of Great Britain, France, Italy and Greece. This commission was at work on August 27 in that region where the boundary was disputed, when the Italian members of the commission were assassinated. Italy accused Greeks of the crime. The Greek government denied the charge. Italy made certain demands upon Greece, threatening penalties if they were not complied with by a certain time. Greece did not comply with the demands. Italy fulfilled her threat. Greece applied to the League of Nations. There the matter rests. What one of the above series of events would have not transpired had America been a member of the League of Nations? Common sense answers the question. America's membership in the league would not have prevented any of the above happenings…"

After settling the Albanian dispute, the League spent the next decade or so dealing with small-scale matters, such as the revolt in and around Memel, a port city on the Baltic Sea. Since most of its citizens were of German descent, it came under Allied supervision following the war, and a disagreement arose about what to do with it. France and Poland wanted to turn it into a sort of international city belonging to no one exclusively, but Lithuania wanted it for itself and invaded in January 1923. The French newspaper, *L'Information*, complained, "Lithuania by seizing the neutral district at Memel and the city of Memel itself is menacing Baltic peace. Where is the money coming from to maintain a big standing army in the little country of Lithuania? The answer is from America, the land of idealism. Money is refused to France so long as she had a military budget. Now we know that charity money which has been sent into Lithuania has been converted into gun powder and machine guns."

It took nearly a year to set up, but in December 1923, the League finally appointed a Commission to look into the matter. The Klaipeda Convention gave Memel to Lithuania on March 8, 1924, declaring, "The British Empire, France, Italy and Japan, signatories with the United States of America, as the Principal Allied and Associated Powers, to the Treaty of Versailles, transfer to Lithuania, subject to the conditions contained in this convention, all the rights and titles ceded to them by Germany in virtue of article 99 of the Treaty of Versailles over the territory lying between the Baltic Sea, the north-eastern frontier of East Prussia (as described in article 28 of the said treaty and as defined in particular by the letter sent on the 18th July. 1921, by the president of the Conference of Ambassadors of the Allied Governments at Paris to the German Ambassador at Paris), and the former frontier between Germany and Russia, the said territory being described in the present convention as 'the Memel Territory.'"

While there were some problems that the League could deal with quickly, others required more attention and more time to resolve. Such was the case with the city of Vilnius, once the capital of Lithuania but also a largely Polish town. The two countries disputed ownership of the city for year, both before and after the League negotiated an agreement between them.

On October 9, 1920, shortly before the League officially commenced activities, Polish General Lucjan Zeligowski had captured the city and declared it to then be the Republic of Central Lithuania, but when the League demanded that Poland evacuate the area, she instead sent in more troops. In spite of the League's demands that a plebiscite be held to allow the citizens to determine their future for themselves, Poland retained control of the area and thus remained in conflict with Lithuania.

Located on the border between Poland and Lithuania, the Republic of Central Lithuania is shown here in green.

Just as they had with other nations, the League was called upon in 1926 to settle a dispute between Iraq and Turkey over the small country of Mosul. Great Britain, who still administered the Mandate for the former, insisted that Mosul should belong to Iraq and thus remain under its control, while Turkey insisted that Mosul should be returned to it since the area had once been part of her own native heartland. The League of Nations concluded on December 16, 1925 that Mosul should remain part of Iraq.

Turkey, however, chose to reject this plan and appealed to the League's Permanent Court of

International Justice. As one reporter explained, "The Fourteenth article of the covenant of the League of Nations contained a clause establishing the new court. Its duty is to determine such questions as are submitted to it, and give advisory opinions on questions submitted by the council or assembly of the league. The Permanent Court of International Justice consists of fifteen members. Candidates for membership are nominated by the various national groups in the Permanent Court of Arbitration.... The two courts interlock in this respect: a majority of the judges of the justice court also are members of the arbitration court. ... The Permanent Court of Arbitration, thus, is neither permanent nor a court. It is a panel, now containing the names of 130 men. The Permanent Court of International Justice is the new world court...which held its first sessions in 1922."

The Court ruled that when the Council's decision was unanimous, the nations involved had to bow to its judgment. In the meanwhile, Britain and Turkey made their own treaty, agreeing that Mosul would go to Iraq.

While it can seem like the League spent most of its time arbitrating disputes between European nations, it was also involved in a number of South American conflicts, particularly the Leticia Dispute between Columbia and Peru. The city of Leticia was given to Columbia by Peru as part of the Salomon-Lozano Treaty of 1922, which gave Columbia access to the Amazon River, a major shipping source in that part of the world. However, a decade later, Peruvian businessmen and land owners raised a small private army and retook Leticia for Peru. After some consideration, President Luis Sanchez Cerro of Peru recognized their work and claimed Leticia for Peru, sending national forces to occupy the city. Over the next several years, the League negotiated an agreement between the two countries that ultimately resulted in Leticia being returned to Columbia, along with a formal letter of apology from Peru.

Chapter 6: It Has Been Decided to Bury It and Start Afresh

"By the Covenant, a definite scheme was set up. It was not, indeed, a full-fledged federation of the world -- far from it -- but it was more than the pious aspiration for peace embodied in the partial alliances which had closed many great struggles. For the first time an organisation was constructed, in essence universal, not to protect the national interests of this or that country -- do let us remember that -- but to abolish war. We saw a new world centre imperfect materially, but enshrining great hopes. An Assembly representing some fifty peace-loving nations, a Council, an international civil service, a world Court of International justice, so often before planned but never created, an International Labour Office to promote better conditions for the workers. And very soon there followed that great apparatus of committees and conferences, striving for an improved civilisation, better international co-operation, a larger redress of grievances and the protection of the helpless and oppressed. Truly this was a splendid programme, the very conception of which was worth all the efforts which it cost. For ten years the League advanced,...but, as we know, it failed in the essential condition of its existence -- namely, the preservation of peace. And so, rightly or wrongly, it has been decided to bury it and start afresh."

That does not mean that the work of twenty years goes for nothing; far from it. All the main ideas…remain." - Robert Cecil, the last Secretary General of the League of Nations

There are few things that threaten peace like economic downturns. While there is always an uptick in domestic violence during times of financial struggle, international threats can also spring up as desperate countries look for ways to feed and house their citizens. As the worldwide prosperity of the 1920s gave way to an international economic depression in the 1930s, countries around the world became restless, looking for more money, resources, and hope.

Nowhere was this more pronounced than in Germany. Defeat in World War I had left it reeling with shame, injured pride, and deep resentment, not to mention racked economic woes. To be fair, the nation had been filled with discontent and problems even before the conflict began, including an extremely poisonous and widespread anti-Semitism which flourished because the Jews were defenseless and thus formed a group upon whom the miserable and destitute could take out their frustrations with impunity. But as a result, the combination of military and economic collapse at the end of the war left Germany subject to widespread economic pain and violent social conflict, the kind of conditions that lead to revolutions much like the one that had swept up Russia in 1917.

The fear, despair, and deprivation of the German people quickly coalesced into action, usually anti-democratic and marked by outbursts of violence. The era "brought with it a 'new wind' in politics throughout Germany […] The wind blew from the trenches, from the schools, from the universities […] Fanned by it, a large number of political and political-military groups developed in postwar Germany […] the new groups […] opposed all existing political groups, institutions, and doctrines, and were to a considerable extent mutually competitive and destructive." (Gordon, 1972, 3).

Throughout all of this, the overarching problem for the Weimar Republic was the economy. The interplay of three factors – war reparations, taxes, and inflation – created a deadly puzzle from which the government ultimately proved unable to extract itself in time. War reparations demanded large amounts of money, but raising taxes infuriated all levels of society to the point of a real threat to oust the current government. The combination dealt a serious blow to the tenuous efforts at recovery made by the prostrate German economy.

Initially, the government's solution was to print vast quantities of money, which removed the need to raise taxes but also led to runaway hyperinflation. A moderate level of inflation would have been constructive, providing the growing capital needed for a modern economy to diversify, create new industries, and generate high-paying jobs, but the inflation rose far beyond this optimal level. That said, the policies did result in a rapid re-industrialization of Germany, which would prove highly useful to Hitler and the Nazi Party in the 1930s, even as one economic catastrophe after another came during the 1920s.

The inflationary process snowballed in a bizarre and unstoppable manner in late 1922 and into 1923, the year the Beer Hall Putsch took place in November. The Germans fell behind on coal shipments to France, which formed a part of their reparations to that country, and as a result, the French and Belgians invaded and seized the Ruhr district in early 1923. The loss of this coal and industrial district was a crippling blow to the already collapsing Germany economy, and extreme hyperinflation resulted. In mid-1922, $1 was worth 1,000 marks, but by the start of 1923, it was worth 4.2 trillion marks.

Naturally, the consequences for ordinary people were devastating. Considering the rise in inflation, it is perhaps astonishing that mayhem and serious attempts at revolution did not occur sooner. Regardless, the conditions were ripe for a man with a cookie-duster mustache who dreamed of a Thousand-Year Reich, the extermination of Jews, and the rise of Germany as a dominant military power. At the moment when Germany was writhing in the fatal grip of hyperinflation and facing the real prospect of mass starvation in late 1923, this man emerged to challenge the world powers and issue the call for Germany's renewal. That man, of course, was Adolf Hitler.

Hitler as a soldier in World War I

Hitler's Nazi Germany would demonstrate the League's utter impotence in the late 1930s, but the League's power actually began to unravel in September 1931 due to the Manchurian Incident. Japan was in the habit of stationing troops near the South Manchurian Railway, a major transportation hub. Looking for an excuse to invade China, the Kwantung Army went and sabotaged the railway, blaming the damage on China. The Army then proceeded to occupy the region with a government of its own creation, christening the area Manchuko. Italy and Germany recognized this false rule, but no one else did, and when China asked the League for help mediating the incident, the officials ruled that Manchuria did indeed belong to China. Undeterred, Japan responded by advancing even further into China and then leaving the League of Nations. Since economic sanctions were useless without the cooperation of the United States and Britain and France too busy with their own problems to offer military aid, the League was hamstrung and ultimately did nothing, allowing Japanese aggression to spread. As French League member Joseph Paul-Boncour later pointed out, "There was the case of Manchuria. The League did nothing but utter verbal protests against Japan's action in attacking an ancient country with a civilisation much older than any of ours which was groping its way towards democracy among the obstacles inherent in its geography and history. We forgot that, just as the revolver-shot of Sarajevo shook the whole world to its foundations, a gun-shot fired on the coast of the Pacific might have its repercussions in Europe. And the proof is that it was the resistance of China -- China, which had been at war since 1931, almost abandoned by the League -- that prevented Japan, the partner of the Axis, from interfering in the affairs of Europe and perhaps changing its face. Manchuria was far off. Ethiopia, and still more Italy, was nearer. In that case, sanctions -- or at any rate economic sanctions -- were decided on, but (if I may employ a popular expression) they were slow-motion sanctions, imposed by driblets. We recoiled before the only two sanctions which would have been effective -- the cutting off of oil supplies and the closing of the Suez Canal. We did enough to irritate Italy and to embarrass her, but not enough to prevent her from accomplishing her conquest."

Picture of a Chinese delegate addressing the League of Nations in 1932 after the Japanese invasion of Manchuria

Paul-Boncour

Japan continued to press further and further into China, and on July 8, 1937, the *Associated Press* reported, "Fighting rages in the western suburbs of this ancient Dragon capital of China between Japanese forces and Chinese General Sung Chen-Yun's 20th army today after a midnight clash between troops conducting secret night maneuvers. Japanese soldiers seized a portion of the railroad from Pelping southward to Hankow and repeatedly attacked the city of Wanplnghslen. There was heavy fighting in the vicinity of the Marble Bridge of Warco Poll, 10 miles west of Pelping. The Chinese were reported to have established their main positions within Wanplnghslen in the face of a reported ultimatum from Japanese troops demanding their immediate surrender. Soldiers of the Chinese army said fighting broke out about midnight when night maneuvering Japanese troops attempted to capture the Marble Bridge across the Vingting river. After a brief skirmish there, Chinese withdrew into Wanplnghslen which the Japanese brought under artillery fire at dawn. Japanese sources denied Wanpingsicn had been being boarded and accused the Chinese of starting the trouble. Japan maintains a garrison of some 700 troops in the Pelplng-Tlanbdii area of North China under its interpretation of the Boxer protocol of 1901 under which the Chinese empire gave principal foreign powers right to use troops to keep the route open between Pelping and the sea."

The Chinese once again asked the League to intervene, and once again the League was unable to do anything.

As Hitler's power increased and the rest of Europe became increasingly nervous, the League tried valiantly but hopelessly to maintain peace, going as far as to encourage Hitler himself to allow his country to join. On September 30, 1938, the wire services out of Europe reported, "The assembly of the League of Nations Friday accepted the principle of separating the league Covenant from the Versailles treaty. The League of Nations was born of the postwar peace pact and the covenant its constitution was written into the Versailles treaty. Approval of separating them, coming a day after the Munich conference on Czechoslovakia, paves the way for erasure of one of Germany's main argument against membership. The assembly accepted the recommendation of a subcommittee for the separation. The governments must ratify the recommendations which, were made in the form of an amendment to the covenant."

This last hope for peace died with Germany's invasion of Poland on September 1, 1939, marking the start of World War II. The League acted quickly to both evacuate its Geneva headquarters and at the same time make sure it could continue to exist, at least in some form.

December 14, 1939 proved to be a watershed day for the League. That day, it expelled the Soviet Union, which had only been a member since 1934, for invading Finland, and the Assembly also temporarily transferred its ruling power to the Secretary General, Lord Cecil, so that he could at least keep the organization's name alive. In the end, this was largely a hollow victory, as the Tehran Conference of 1943, attended by the "Big Three" of Franklin Roosevelt, Winston Churchill, and Joseph Stalin, came up with the idea of a new, and stronger, peacekeeping force that would come to be known as the United Nations.

As Roosevelt's brainchild, it was the American president who suggested that the active arm of the organization be "the Four Policemen": the USA, USSR, UK, and China. Stalin agreed with much of the framework in principle, but stated that China likely would not possess the strength after the war to assist. He also noted that the "Policemen" must hold a series of strong points, putting Germany and Japan at too much of a disadvantage to attempt military adventurism again. Roosevelt agreed with everything Stalin said.

The Yalta Conference, held in early 1945 as the war in Europe was clearly drawing to a close, further cemented the idea. At Yalta, Roosevelt made clear he wanted to create the United Nations as an improved version of the League, headed by the United States, the United Kingdom, the Soviet Union, and Chiang Kai-Shek's Nationalist China. Though many other countries would hold seats in the UN, Roosevelt envisioned these four as holding the senior position, making them able to pressure the other countries (and each other) into avoiding conflict-generating situations. Seeking to avoid Wilson's failure, Roosevelt also proposed that the UN headquarters would be in the United States, increasing the organization's authority with the military and industrial power of America.

Churchill, Roosevelt, and Stalin at the Yalta Conference

In response to Roosevelt's suggestion, Stalin suggested that the larger powers (the USSR, USA, and Britain) should essentially govern the postwar world, and the small nations be permitted to offer their opinions but not interfere with the plans of the major countries. Churchill, for once, agreed with the Soviet strongman, at least in spirit, famously stating, "The eagle should let the small birds sing and care not wherefore they sang." This statement paraphrased part of a speech delivered in William Shakespeare's *Titus Andronicus*. Roosevelt, however, still preferred the notion of all the "birds" having an equal voice in decision-making, the system that was ultimately actually adopted.

Of course, the wily Stalin wouldn't let that point go quietly. In announcing that they fully accepted the Security Council's voting process for the United Nations, Soviet officials stated flatly that the Soviets would need two, or possibly three, additional seats in the UN to represent the most important of its 16 republics. The Americans balked, knowing the republics had no independence whatsoever from the dictatorship in Moscow; the measure simply aimed to grant the Soviet Union extra seats and votes. Roosevelt, nonplussed, scribbled a handwritten note saying, "This is not so good" and gave it to another American official. Ultimately, the president resorted to the inevitable technique used throughout the Yalta Conference – a postponement. He suggested that a commission meet in March to iron out the details of the United Nations and create a charter. The UN itself would likely not form until approximately half a year after the charter's acceptance.

As for the League of Nations, which had been completely sidelined, it met for one last time on April 18, 1946, and in his closing remarks, Secretary General Cecil, who had stood alone throughout the war, told the audience, "On May 25th, 1937, before the Council of the League of Nations, took the following oath: 'I solemnly undertake to exercise in all loyalty, discretion and conscience the functions that have been entrusted to me as an official of the Secretariat of the League of Nations, to discharge my functions and to regulate my conduct with the interests of the League alone in view and not to seek or receive instructions from any Government or other authority external to the Secretariat.' I have tried to live up to this declaration during the past nine years. ... The work of the League is unmistakably printed on the social, economic and humanitarian life of the world. But above all that, a great advance was made in the international organisation of peace.... Believe me, there is no safety except in peace, and peace cannot be maintained merely and solely by national armaments, however necessary they may be, by each nation seeking safety for itself. Let us, then, boldly state that aggression, wherever it occurs and however it may be defended, is an international crime, that it is the duty of every peace-loving State to resist it, and to employ whatever force maybe necessary to crush it.... Education in the largest sense is necessary. Everywhere organisations should exist for that purpose, whether supported by the State or drawing their strength from the conviction and enthusiasms of individuals. I venture very respectfully to press upon my hearers that here is a great work for peace in which all can participate, resting not only on the narrow interests of our own nations but even more on those great principles of right and wrong on which nations, like individuals, depend. The League is dead. Long live the United Nations."

With that, the League of Nation's Assembly passed a resolution that read, "With effect from the day following the close of the present session of the Assembly [i.e., April 19], the League of Nations shall cease to exist except for the sole purpose of the liquidation of its affairs as provided in the present resolution." The *Associated Press* reported, "The League of Nations ended its existence today. Delegates of 34 nations, outnumbered by gallery spectators, answered 'yes' late in the afternoon to a resolution providing: 'With effect from the day following the close of the present session of the assembly, the league of Nations shall cease to exist except for the sole purpose of the liquidation of its affairs.' Thus the first major peace organization of the century expired 26 years, three months and eight days after its founding it was conceived by Woodrow

Wilson, but never was joined by the United States."

Even at the end, despite the fact the League of Nations had taken the remarkable step of officially dissolving itself, some of the people who had worked so hard to make it a success refused to accept that it was a complete failure. In the wake of the UN's establishment, Paul-Boncour said of the defunct League, "Our balance-sheet is not altogether unfavourable. Deterioration set in on the day when, imperialism having again broken loose in the world, those precepts of the Covenant whose application would have afforded the only possible basis of a peace honourable for all were offered up as a first sacrifice to the myth of appeasement... In the essential task of maintaining peace it succeeded during a number of years. It succeeded as long as Governments, and particularly the Governments of the Great Powers, put their faith in it and animated and fortified it by their own strength of purpose and as long as, in the background, there was the latent possibility that their force would be put at the service of its decisions. During a number of years, in the period following the peace treaties, the League of Nations settled various grave disputes -- Memel, the Aaland Islands, Upper Silesia and the dispute between Greece and Bulgaria -- all of them involving areas which might have become battlefields if the League had not settled the disputes in their initial stages. It is, indeed, the very success it achieved that caused the disputes to be minimised and that makes us forget what it accomplished. For years it prevented the dispute between Poland and Lithuania from degenerating into war; for years it prevented Germany from seizing Danzig, which she always coveted but whose independence was essential to the free access of Poland to the sea; for years it prevented Balkan rivalries from degenerating into war over Albania, the Dobrudja and all those problems constantly surging up in countries where successive waves of migration have sometimes made frontiers uncertain."

The League of Nations archive in Geneva

Online Resources

Other books about 20th century history by Charles River Editors

Other books about World War I history by Charles River Editors

Other books about the League of Nations on Amazon

Bibliography

Henig, Ruth B, ed. (1973). *The League of Nations*. Oliver and Boyd.

Knock, Thomas J (1995). To End All Wars: Woodrow Wilson and the Quest for a New World Order. Princeton University Press.

Northedge, F.S (1986). *The League of Nations: Its Life and Times, 1920–1946*. Holmes & Meier.

Raffo, P (1974). *The League of Nations*. The Historical Association.

Scott, George (1973). *The Rise and Fall of the League of Nations*. Hutchinson & Co LTD.

Made in the USA
Middletown, DE
06 December 2019